CHRISTIANS AND THE PUBLIC SQUARE

Study by Lee Canipe
Commentary by Brett Younger

Free downloadable Teaching Guide for this study available at
NextSunday.com/teachingguides

NextSunday Resources
6316 Peake Road
Macon, Georgia 31210-3960
1-800-747-3016
©2015 by NextSunday Resources

TABLE OF CONTENTS

Christians and the Public Square

Study Introduction 1

Lesson 1 Dual Citizenship
          Jeremiah 29:4-7; Matthew 22:15-22
          Study 3
          Commentary 11

Lesson 2 Bold Witness
          Amos 7:10-15; Acts 4:13-22
          Study 19
          Commentary 27

Lesson 3 Power Corrupts
          Daniel 3:8-12, 16-18; Revelation 13:1-10
          Study 35
          Commentary 43

Lesson 4 Prayer for Rulers
          Psalm 72:1-7; 1 Timothy 2:1-4
          Study 51
          Commentary 59

HOW TO USE THIS STUDY

NextSunday Resources Adult Bible Studies are designed to help adults study Scripture seriously within the context of the larger Christian tradition and, through that process, find their faith renewed, challenged, and strengthened. We study the Scriptures because we believe they affect our current lives in important ways. Each study contains the following three components:

Study Guide

Each study guide lesson is arranged in four movements:

Reflecting recalls a contemporary story, anecdote, example, or illustration to help us anticipate the session's relevance in our lives.

Studying is centered on giving the biblical material in-depth attention while often surrounding it with helpful insights from theology, ethics, church history, and other areas.

Understanding helps us find relevant connections between our lives and the biblical message.

What About Me? provides brief statements that help unite life issues with the meaning of the biblical text.

Commentary

Each study guide lesson is accompanied by an additional, in-depth commentary on the biblical material. Written by a different author than the study guide, each commentary gives the opportunity for learners to approach the Scripture text from a separate but complementary viewpoint.

Teaching Guide

In addition to the provided study guide and commentary, *NextSunday Resources* also provides a *free* downloadable teaching guide, available at NextSunday.com. Each teaching guide gives the teacher tools for focusing on the content of each study guide lesson through additional commentary and Bible background information. Through teacher helps and teaching options, each teaching guide also provides substance for variety and choice in the preparation of each lesson.

NextSunday
Resources

STUDY INTRODUCTION

Like it or not, it's election time again in the United States, which means partisan passions are probably already running hot, sometimes to the point of boiling over into angry arguments. Unfortunately, Christians are not immune to this reality. Our church rolls contain Democrats, Republicans, and Independents, as well as members of other political parties. All of these folks love Jesus. They also love their country and have opinions about how it ought to be run. Not surprisingly, these folks don't always agree with each other. Our political differences, however, must never be allowed to trump our Christian fellowship.

Politics and faith are tricky areas for Christians to negotiate. The First Amendment to the Constitution guarantees religious freedom for all Americans. Some have argued through the years this means, in part, that people of faith must keep their religious convictions to themselves when participating in public discourse. Such a position not only ignores the rich history of religiously inspired reform in this country (such as the movements *against* slavery and, a century later, *for* civil rights), it also results in what Richard John Neuhaus once described as a "naked public square," a morally and intellectually impoverished culture stripped bare of all religious influence.

The truth is that Christians are neither called by God to be silent in the public square, nor does the law prohibit us from speaking up and speaking out as guided by the Holy Spirit. Yet still, as Christians who are also citizens, questions abound: How do we know when to speak and when to be quiet? How do we distinguish between faithful and unfaithful forms of civic engagement? How do we give Caesar his due while giving our all to God? God's people have long wrestled with these issues. Fortunately, they've left a record of both their questions and their answers. With the Bible as our guide, then, let's plunge ahead into the often-contested public square as citizens and as Christians seeking to do what is good and right in the name of Jesus Christ.

DUAL CITIZENSHIP
Jeremiah 29:4-7; Matthew 22:15-22

Central Question

What can I do to improve my community?

Scripture

Jeremiah 29:4-7 4 Thus says the Lord of hosts, the God of Israel, to all the exiles whom I have sent into exile from Jerusalem to Babylon: 5 Build houses and live in them; plant gardens and eat what they produce. 6 Take wives and have sons and daughters; take wives for your sons, and give your daughters in marriage, that they may bear sons and daughters; multiply there, and do not decrease. 7 But seek the welfare of the city where I have sent you into exile, and pray to the Lord on its behalf, for in its welfare you will find your welfare.

Matthew 22:15-22 15 Then the Pharisees went and plotted to entrap him in what he said. 16 So they sent their disciples to him, along with the Herodians, saying, "Teacher, we know that you are sincere, and teach the way of God in accordance with truth, and show deference to no one; for you do not regard people with partiality. 17 Tell us, then, what you think. Is it lawful to pay taxes to the emperor, or not?" 18 But Jesus, aware of their malice, said, "Why are you putting me to the test, you hypocrites? 19 Show me the coin used for the tax." And they brought him a denarius. 20 Then he said to them, "Whose head is this, and whose title?" 21 They answered, "The emperor's." Then he said to them, "Give therefore to the emperor the things that are the emperor's, and to God the things that are God's." 22 When they heard this, they were amazed; and they left him and went away.

Reflecting

In the movie *Chariots of Fire* (Warner Brothers, 1981), British runner Eric Liddell faces a quandary at the 1924 Olympics. A devout Christian, he believes that the Sabbath is for rest and belongs exclusively to God. The problem? His race falls on a Sunday. After much soul-searching, Liddell withdraws from competition, forsaking his shot at Olympic glory in order to obey God.

When the British Olympic officials (a group that includes the Prince of Wales) learn of Liddell's decision, they engage in some polite, but high-powered, arm-twisting. "In my day," growls the Olympic committee chair, "it was king first, God after." Liddell, however, remains true to his convictions: No running on Sunday. The prince then takes a different tack. "We share a common loyalty," he says. "There are times when we're asked to make sacrifices in the name of that loyalty. Without them our allegiance is worthless. As I see it, for you this is one of those times."

Liddell exhales slowly, then addresses his king's eldest son. "God knows I love my country," he says, "but I can't make that sacrifice."

Eric Liddell's decision was difficult, but at least the alternatives were clear. That is not always the case. Insofar as we Christians enjoy citizenship in heaven and in our own countries here on earth, God and Caesar make competing—and, Jesus teaches, legitimate—claims on us.

Unfortunately, the proper dividing line between these two sets of claims is rarely highlighted in flashing neon. As with most moral challenges, it's easier to *talk about* separating what belongs to God from what belongs to Caesar than it is to *do* it. When negotiating the overlapping responsibilities of dual citizenship, however, the prophet Jeremiah reminds us that the Lord expects us to make the places where we live better, investing in the common good of our communities and our nation—but always on God's terms.

Studying

Let's begin with our passage from Matthew, which has long served as a launching pad for conversations about God, Caesar, and the dual citizenship Christians live out in this world. Determined to discredit Jesus and undermine his authority as a teacher, the Pharisees lay a trap for him, hoping to entangle him in his own words. In fact, this discussion about paying taxes is the first of three controversial questions lobbed at—and successfully parried by—Jesus in Matthew 22. Jesus' response to this cleverly posed, yet dangerous, question displays great wisdom.

Most Jews detested paying taxes to support the Roman government that ruled over them as an occupying power. Not only were the Romans foreigners, but they were pagans as well. Moreover, they demanded that taxes be paid in Roman currency, which typically featured both the emperor's image and his quasi-divine title. It was all too much for loyal, religiously scrupulous Jews to stomach. Nobody liked paying the taxes but, at the same time, nobody dared complain too loudly for fear of how the Romans might respond.

So, the question posed in verse 17—"Is it lawful to pay taxes to the emperor, or not?"—puts Jesus in the midst of a dilemma. Either he condemns the tax and risks getting into trouble with the Romans or he endorses the tax and the crowd accuses him of selling out to the bad guys.

A common denarius coin used to pay the Roman tax mentioned in Matthew 22:17 was worth approximately one day's wage for a laborer. It featured the image of the emperor, Caesar Tiberius, and carried the inscription "Tiberius Caesar, august [i.e., revered] son of the divine Augustus and high priest."

With great dexterity, however, Jesus offers a third option. He asks his inquisitors for a Roman coin, which they quickly produce. Pointing to the coin, Jesus asks them: "Whose head is this, and whose title?" (v. 20). "The emperor's," they reply. Well, then, says Jesus, "give therefore to the emperor the things that are the emperor's, and to God the things that are God's" (v. 21). Matthew tells us that Jesus' answer amazes his antagonists and sends them away, no doubt scratching their heads over how they managed to pull defeat from the jaws of victory.

It's tempting to turn Jesus' clever response to a difficult question into an iron-clad rule for settling any and all conflicts concerning our obligations to God and Caesar. Unfortunately, this principle doesn't always help us distinguish what rightfully belongs to the one from what rightfully belongs to the other, as though our lives could ever be so neatly compartmentalized. If anything, Jesus is saying that it *all* belongs to God. After all, what good Jew would ever dispute the sweeping claim of Psalm 24:1 that "the earth is the Lord's and all that is in it, the world, and those who live in it"? That certainly doesn't leave much left over for Caesar!

As long as we understand, however, that our bodies and souls belong exclusively to God, then Jesus doesn't rule out the possibility that emperors (or any other earthly rulers) might make legitimate claims on us as citizens, especially when it comes to contributing to the welfare of our communities. In fact, the Bible tells us that regardless of where we live, God expects us to work there for the common good—even if where we live now is not, ultimately, our true home.

These are the instructions that God sends through the prophet Jeremiah to the people living in exile far from home. King Nebuchadnezzar conquered Judah and carted its best and brightest citizens off to Babylon. These Jews, trapped in a pagan culture, are, quite literally, strangers in a strange land—aliens in the truest sense of the word. They don't belong in Babylon, yet there they are.

Under the circumstances, God's people could have chosen one of two paths: rebellion or resignation. The Lord, however, has other plans. Build houses, God says. Plant gardens and enjoy their produce. Marry and start families. In other words, put down deep roots and invest yourselves in this strange land for as long as you are there. Do your best to make it a good place to live and pray specifically for its welfare, God commands, "for in its welfare you will find your welfare" (v. 7).

We might be forgiven if we detect a note of cynicism in this exhortation. After all, the exiles' welfare is dependent on that of Babylon. Therefore, we might interpret their motivation as self-centered. But, as Fretheim explains, there are also theological issues at stake:

> The exiles are not only to seek the well-being of Babylon, they are to pray to God on behalf of the city. Such prayers assume that God desires to be present and active in a focused way in the lives of the exiles and in the lives of the Babylonians. This is the image of a Creator God who is active in the world even in the lives of people who do not acknowledge him as Lord. God's work will be effective among them for good, even though they may not realize that God is so involved. And these positive results will redound to the benefit of the Babylonians them-selves, and not just to the Israelites among them. And so, even if the motivation is enlightened self-interest, the benefits that would accrue to the Babylonians will multiply across the entire society, and through the Babylonians to other cultures. (410)

It's worth noting here that God's understanding of the common good is quite broad. God doesn't tell the Jewish exiles to work and pray for the welfare of those who look, worship, vote, and earn a living like they do. Instead, God says they should work and pray for the good of the whole city—and that means everybody.

Understanding

There are certain basic goods that all people cherish. Regardless of race, creed, or culture, we consider these things vital to a sense of well-being: nutritious food; clean water; a decent education for our children; safe places to live, work, and play; the opportunity to earn an honest living; and access to adequate medical care. If we believe that God not only created all people, but also loves us enough to send Jesus to die for our sake, then it's not hard to understand God's concern for the welfare of our communities. Simply put, the Bible tells us that God wants everyone to flourish and has called us to work toward that end. Strong, safe, healthy communities benefit everyone.

When Caesar acts in ways that promote the kind of strong, safe, and healthy communities that are pleasing to the Lord, then God's people are right to support those efforts. It's important to remember, though, that human welfare was God's concern long before it was Caesar's. Furthermore, because our true citizenship is in heaven, we are called to put everything we have and everything we are at God's disposal to be used for God's purposes.

This means that when it comes to seeking the welfare of the places where we live, we take our cues from God, not Caesar. Christians can't simply shrug and say, "I've done *my* part by paying my taxes," because, as Jesus makes clear, what we owe Caesar represents but a drop in the bucket of what God expects from us.

This world is not our home, and we Christians must never forget where—and to whom—we truly belong, lest we confuse God's will for our lives with Caesar's. Even so, the Bible makes it clear that while we are here, there is plenty of holy, blessed work to do pursuing the common good for all of God's children in those places where we live.

What About Me?

• *It's easier to separate sacred and secular in theory than it is in practice.* The reality is that our lives cannot be compartmentalized with respect to our commitments to the sacred and the secular. Paul tells us in Romans 12:1-2 that everything we think, say, and do is an act of worship in the eyes of God. Our actions are either acceptable to God or they're not. The same goes for our priorities. Insisting that "Caesar made me do it" does not relieve us of our responsibility to obey God's commandments.

• *Caesar has a purpose.* In Romans 13, Paul argues for civil government as something God instituted for the proper ordering of society. Christians may legitimately disagree about the proper roles or limitations of government, but there is no room in Scripture for advocating anarchism. The Bible is quite consistent that God's people must pay their taxes to support the common good—even if we're not always happy about it!

• *Be the change you want to see.* Anyone can complain about what's wrong with the world. People who make a positive difference are those who are willing to take action and lead by example. The efforts of one individual may seem pitifully small in comparison to the challenges that our communities face, but until someone recognizes a problem and does something about it, nothing will ever change.

• *Where do I start? How do I start?* Different people feel passionately about different things, and, for better or worse, most communities have many different needs. Usually there is no shortage of places to invest ourselves for the sake of the common good. Paying attention to what stirs our hearts, whether it's educating children or revitalizing downtown, is the first step in getting involved. The Holy Spirit tends to lead us toward the needs that God has equipped us to meet, so take the Spirit's nudges seriously. Then, start asking questions, attending meetings, and talking with neighbors, fellow church members, and parents at school. Chances are, others have noticed the same needs and opportunities and, with encouragement, will pitch in to make their community a better place to live.

Resources

Terence E. Fretheim, *Jeremiah*, Smyth & Helwys Bible Commentary (Macon GA: Smyth & Helwys, 2002).

Ben Witherington III, *Matthew*, Smyth & Helwys Bible Commentary (Macon GA: Smyth & Helwys, 2006).

DUAL CITIZENSHIP
Jeremiah 29:4-7; Matthew 22:15-22

God and Country

Mark Twain once said that a citizen could not be a Christian and a patriot at the same time. He argued that "Christian citizen" is an oxymoron representing two irreconcilable loyalties. Many Christians disagree with Twain, but being both a faithful Christian and a patriotic citizen is, at times, challenging.

What should Christians do if asked to participate in a war they believe is unjust? How should we respond to churches taking government funds?

What should we think about federal judges who hang the Ten Commandments in their courtrooms? How should we feel about the government inserting the words "under God" into the Pledge of Allegiance, then taking them out, and then putting them back in? Francis Bellamy, a Baptist minister, wrote the original Pledge of Allegiance in 1892. He not only didn't include the words "under God" in the original pledge, he also refused to add the words "with equality" because he didn't think the country was fair to women or African Americans (John Baer, *The Pledge of Allegiance* [Annapolis MD: Free State Press, 1992]).

How should we react to government-sponsored prayer? Do we want Congress teaching our children how to pray? How should we feel about hollow political references to an innocuous God? Does civil religion get in the way of real Christianity?

Sincere people of faith disagree. The frustration that surrounds church-and-state issues runs deep. It can be confusing. We assume it used to be simpler. Maybe it has always been complicated.

God and Someone Else's Country? (Jer 29:4-7)

Over 2,500 years ago, on the other side of the world, a powerful and ruthless enemy attacked the little nation of Judah. The Babylonian army, commanded by Nebuchadnezzar, was conquering everything in its path. The Jewish people retreated to Jerusalem. Eventually they ran out of food. They could no longer defend themselves.

In 598 BC, many of the remaining citizens of Jerusalem were forced on a long march to Babylon. None of them would see their homeland again. Their world had ended. Their home was a pile of rubble.

Jeremiah 29 contains excerpts from four letters between the community that remained in Judah and the Babylonian exiles. The first is from Jeremiah to the exiles (29:1-15). This letter seems to have been written when the exiles had only been there for a short time and might correspond to around 595-594 BC when there was political unrest in Babylon that made the deportees think they might be returning to Judah soon (R. E. Clements, *Jeremiah*, Interpretation [Atlanta: John Knox, 1988] 170).

This correspondence between Jeremiah and the exiles is surprising. Apparently, Babylonian officials wanted to facilitate communication between the two groups (v. 3). Royal emissaries carried the letter from Judah to Babylon. Jeremiah begins with the disappointing word that God has done this: "Thus says the LORD of hosts, the God of Israel, to all the exiles whom I have sent into exile" (v. 4). The people needed to find life in their new home that did not feel like home and were instructed to "build houses and live in them; plant gardens and eat what they produce" (v. 5). Jeremiah says they should "take wives and have sons and daughters" (v. 6). The divine blessings of children and well-being were to continue in exile. Jeremiah calls on the people to "multiply...and...not decrease." They were not to miss the life they had by looking back at the life they used to have.

Jeremiah even tells the exiles to "seek the welfare of the city" and "pray to the LORD on its behalf" (v. 7). Imagine your pastor calling on a church member imprisoned in North Korea to pray for the North Korean government because "in its welfare you will find your welfare" (v. 7). The exiles were to pray for the enemy that brought about Judah's downfall, to pray sincerely for Babylon's deliverance from danger.

Jeremiah offers a word of grace. This might have been a much different letter if the confrontational Jeremiah had been there himself. He recognized that resisting the Babylonians would be dangerous for his friends. Prophets who predicted the downfall of Babylon could be executed (v. 21), so Jeremiah counsels acceptance. He knows that those taken to Babylon will not return to their homeland. "Seventy years" (v. 10) signifies a lifetime. Hope cannot be based on naïve patriotic expectations that God will defeat their enemies.

Patriotism and nationalism are so often intertwined that some may not even recognize that people of faith live in exile, far from their true home. Jeremiah ends up pointing to a religion of the heart rather than political power: "When you search for me, you will find me; if you seek me with all your heart" (v. 13). The period of waiting in exile could be years of spiritual growth. We, too, are to pray for the good of whatever city in which we find ourselves exiled.

Church and State (Mt 22:15-22)

Two thousand years ago, some experts on church and state came to interrogate Jesus. The Pharisees, who had already decided to kill Jesus (Mt 12:14), resented the Roman occupation but accepted it as a necessary evil. The Herodians were a secular pro-Roman political party. The Pharisees and Herodians had different views on almost everything, but they agreed that Jesus' way would be the end of what they loved most. They wanted to keep their conference tables, agendas, and Italian suits. They wanted to show that Jesus' insistence on complete devotion to God alone was unrealistic, so they came up with a plan to make him look foolish.

An alliance between these two groups was about as likely as the Tea Party and the ACLU working together, but both groups knew how to ask what Sarah Palin calls a "gotcha question." They throw out a compliment before pulling out the knife. The lawyer's flattery is over the top: "Teacher, we know that you are sincere, and teach the way of God in accordance with truth, and show deference to no one; for you do not regard people with partiality. Tell us, then, what you think. Is it lawful to pay taxes to the emperor, or not?" (vv. 16-17).

The question could be paraphrased, "Does the Torah permit the payment of taxes to Caesar or not?" If Jesus argues against paying the tax, he could be accused of anti-Roman activity. If he supports the tax, he will lose popularity. His answer would either alienate nationalists or make him subject to arrest. This tax referred to the Roman head-tax, which was instituted in AD 6 when Judea became a Roman province. This census triggered the nationalism that finally became the Zealot movement, which began the disastrous war of 66–70 (M. Eugene Boring, "The Gospel of Matthew," *New Interpreter's Bible Commentary* [Nashville TN: Abingdon, 1995] 420).

They might have expected some fierce theological ping-pong, but Jesus was not born yesterday. He didn't want to play. In effect he said, "You hypocrites, what do you think you're doing? Do you really think I'm going to fall for that? You don't care what I think. You just want me in more trouble than I'm already in."

Instead of taking the bait and discussing politics, Jesus, who does not have a coin himself, calls for a Roman coin (v. 19). The coin contained an image and inscription considered blasphemous by many Jews: "Tiberius Caesar, august son of the divine Augustus, high priest" (Douglas Hare, *Matthew*, Interpretation [Louisville KY: John Knox, 1993] 254). Right there in the temple, Jesus' adversaries promptly produce a coin that violates their religion! The hypocrisy is clear: the Pharisees do business with Caesar's coins.

Jesus goes beyond their original question and declares that while what is God's must be given to God, "Give therefore to the emperor the things that are the emperor's, and to God the things that are God's" (v. 21). This is not a division of the world into two kingdoms. The kingdom of God embraces all of life. Jesus is not saying, "Equal respect must be given to Caesar and God." Loyalty to God is a different category. The second half practically annuls the first by preempting it.

Caesar's role is vastly inferior. Followers of Christ owe full allegiance to God alone. When the early church read this story they knew how hard this was. When they were forced to choose between God and Caesar, they ended up in the coliseum with the lions.

Citizens of One Kingdom

If Jesus had been willing to give to Caesar what belonged to God, he would not have been crucified. The government wanted Jesus to be silent, but he kept talking about God's grace for all people everywhere. In this text, Jesus said, "Give...to God the things that are God's." Later that week, the government executed Jesus because he was a dangerous person who was loyal to God and not the state.

Believers are not citizens of two kingdoms. Christians have one king. We owe all of our allegiance to God. Those first Christians who chose to die rather than submit to Caesar's kingship would be disappointed to hear Christians today talk about being citizens of two kingdoms. How would they feel to hear Christians pledging allegiance to a country rather than Christ alone? Jehovah's Witnesses will not say a pledge to their country because they believe their only allegiance belongs to God. They have a point.

When we act as good citizens, it should be because we are living out our faith and not because we owe allegiance to the government. Martin Luther King Jr. said the church is "the conscience of the state. It must be the guide and the critic of the state, and never its tool" (*Church State Council*, http://church-state.org/index.php?id=166). The church has always struggled with what is Caesar's and what is God's. The best thing the government can do for Christianity is leave it alone.

Our country has been a beacon of religious freedom. People of every faith get the same vote—whether they're Christians, Jews, or anything else. Together we give thanks for a prosperous land. We celebrate the good things about America, support our nation, and pray for its leaders. We glory in the wisdom of our Founding Fathers and give thanks for the sacrifices that made their dreams come true. We are so grateful for our country that we work to make it better. Our nation needs our help to live out the dream inscribed on the Statue of Liberty, "Give me your tired, your poor, your huddled masses yearning to breathe free."

Every once in a while you read an editorial that says citizens should vote their own self-interest. Christians should never do that. We vote not in our self-interest, but in the interest of those who need our help.

Our government always needs reforming, always needs to be taken from the self-seekers and given to those who are in danger of being left behind. We work for our country to grow in her generosity, care for the elderly, improve our schools, and protect the environment. We work to shield our children in an increasingly violent society. We keep asking whether the right to bear arms really means that we create a society where violent people are better armed than the police.

We act out of Christian convictions when we pray for our enemies and argue against sowing seeds of hate. More than at any other time in our history, our country is tempted by its power. Material and military preeminence are a danger. We are tempted to believe that we are beyond judgment. We need people of faith to call our country to act redemptively toward other nations. God calls Christians beyond love of country to love the whole world. Kenneth Calder said, "To seek God's blessing for America and not for the world fails to recognize the wideness in God's mercy and the expanse of God's love" ("God Bless America—and the World," http://archives.umc.org/umns/commentary_archive.asp?ptid=&story={3D11788C-C541-482D-8FD4-B049414CB1F4}&mid=894).

According to Jesus, faith in God is more important than love of country. Christians believe not only in the separation of church and state, but in the superiority of church to state. Our faith must determine our politics and never the other way around. Our country's wonderful history is short when compared to the story of God's grace. God was here long before our country. God will be present long after nations pass from the scene. Our allegiance belongs to God alone.

Notes

Notes

2

BOLD WITNESS

Amos 7:10-15; Acts 4:13-22

Central Question

When must I speak out? When is silence the better option?

Scripture

Amos 7:10-15 10 Then Amaziah, the priest of Bethel, sent to King Jeroboam of Israel, saying, "Amos has conspired against you in the very center of the house of Israel; the land is not able to bear all his words. 11 For thus Amos has said, 'Jeroboam shall die by the sword, and Israel must go into exile away from his land.'" 12 And Amaziah said to Amos, "O seer, go, flee away to the land of Judah, earn your bread there, and prophesy there; 13 but never again prophesy at Bethel, for it is the king's sanctuary, and it is a temple of the kingdom." 14 Then Amos answered Amaziah, "I am no prophet, nor a prophet's son; but I am a herdsman, and a dresser of sycamore trees, 15 and the Lord took me from following the flock, and the Lord said to me, 'Go, prophesy to my people Israel.'"

Acts 4:13-22 13 Now when they saw the boldness of Peter and John and realized that they were uneducated and ordinary men, they were amazed and recognized them as companions of Jesus. 14 When they saw the man who had been cured standing beside them, they had nothing to say in opposition. 15 So they ordered them to leave the council while they discussed the matter with one another. 16 They said, "What will we do with them? For it is obvious to all who live in Jerusalem that a notable sign has been done through them; we cannot deny it. 17 But to keep it from spreading further among the people, let us warn them to speak no more to anyone in this name." 18 So they called them and ordered them not to speak or teach at all in the name of Jesus. 19 But Peter and John answered them, "Whether it is right in God's sight to listen to you rather than to God, you must judge; 20 for we cannot keep from speaking about what we have seen and heard." 21 After threatening them again, they let them go, finding no way to punish them because of the people, for all of them praised God for what had happened. 22 For the man on whom this sign of healing had been performed was more than forty years old.

Reflecting

A journalist once asked N. T. Wright, an Anglican bishop and New Testament scholar, how he understood the relationship between religion and politics. The church's message to those in positions of earthly power, Wright responded, is fairly straight-forward: "We are urging you to do justice, and we're going to hold your feet to the fire and go on reminding you when you're getting it wrong and congratulating you when you get it right" (Meacham).

Congratulations, of course, are always welcome. Political leaders are usually quite grateful for the moral authority they gain by associating themselves with friendly pastors and adoring congregations. No one ever got in trouble with the powers that be by celebrating their wisdom and virtue.

Congratulating those in power is easy. Holding their feet to the fire is not. Throughout history, those who tell inconvenient truths to people in positions of authority tend to find themselves under pressure, either to change their tunes or to shut their mouths. As Wright suggests, however, part of our witness as Christians is to tell the truth, sometimes to people who have no desire to hear it and have a vested interest in silencing it.

> **?** How can Christians distinguish between our personal political inclinations and things that God would have us do or say with respect to the pressing matters of our times?

The Scripture passages in today's lesson provide glimpses of both the power and the perils of telling God's truth to those who don't want to hear it. Speaking up and speaking out certainly require a great deal of courage and a willingness to suffer the assaults to one's reputation that come with voicing an unpopular opinion.

As we study these verses, though, it's important to remember that neither Amos nor Peter and John necessarily *wanted* to be in this uncomfortable position. Rather, they speak out of obedience to the call of God. In other words, all three speak not because *they* have something to say, but because God has something to say through them. The distinction is crucial.

Studying

We begin with the prophet Amos, whose preaching shook the pillars of power at Bethel, where King Jeroboam II of Israel maintained one of his two royal sanctuaries. What did Amos say? Quite a lot, actually.

Beginning with Amos 5, the prophet details Israel's sins, charging that the rich and powerful have indulged in luxury, perverted justice, and prospered by taking advantage of the poor. What's more, these same Israelites have maintained a façade of religious piety while behaving in an unholy manner—a brazen hypocrisy that God finds particularly offensive. Because of Israel's injustice and unrighteousness, the Lord declares that there will be a heavy price to pay: "The sanctuaries of Israel shall be laid waste, and I will rise against the house of Jeroboam with the sword" (Am 7:9).

The name "Amos" comes from a Hebrew word meaning "to carry a load." Given the Old Testament prophet's difficult vocation and challenging message, Martin Luther believed that Amos more than lived up to his name. "He can well be called Amos," wrote the German reformer, "that is, 'a burden,' one who is hard to get along with and irritating." (Limburg, 81)

This last message finally forces Jeroboam's inner circle to take notice. Amaziah, the chief priest at Bethel, informs the king of Amos's proclamation. Four aspects of the priest's missive deserve attention. First, notice how Amaziah describes the prophet's

action in treasonous terms: "Amos has *conspired* against you," he says (v. 10), suggesting that any criticism of the king—however legitimate—is tantamount to disloyalty. Second, the priest implies that Amos is preying on people's fears, for "the land is not able to bear all his words" (v. 10). Third, by attributing the disturbing words to Amos alone—"For thus *Amos* has said" (v. 11)—Amaziah undermines the prophet's authority as the Lord's messenger. Fourth, Amaziah's account of Amos's declaration mentions the coming punishment in embellished terms but ignores the sins that have provoked God's wrath in the first place.

Amaziah's answer to Amos is a textbook smear campaign that questions the prophet's patriotism, accuses him of fear-mongering, attacks his credibility, and misrepresents his message. The powers that be know how to play the game, especially when their own self-preservation is on the line. Then, in an effort to silence the unwanted prophet and prevent further embarrassing outbursts, Amaziah commands Amos to leave town and never come back. Other people in other places might want to hear you, says the priest, but the good, loyal, God-fearing folks here in Bethel most certainly do not (vv. 12-13).

Amos, however, refuses to turn the confrontation into a personal challenge for, to him, there's nothing *personal* about it. "I am no prophet," he says, but rather a herdsman and a dresser of sycamore trees (v. 14). Amos then recalls how God called him to leave his flock and go prophesy to Israel (v. 15). In other words, Amos says, "This is not about me." It's about what God wants to say and what God's people need to hear. For Amos, truth-telling begins with obedience.

We find a similar dynamic at work in Acts 4:13-22, where Peter and John stand before the ruling Jewish council in Jerusalem. They've been hauled into court because of their miraculous healings in Jesus' name (Acts 3:1-10). Their bold proclamations of Jesus' gospel (Acts 3:11-26) have finally gotten on the Jerusalem authorities' collective last nerve (Acts 4:1-3). To the council, the two apostles appear to be fairly ordinary, even uneducated, men, which makes their remarkable behavior all the more amazing (v. 13). Usually in these circumstances, the first order of business for the council might be to discredit the apostles' work—to imply that their healing of a crippled beggar was somehow a hoax. But the fact that the healed beggar is standing with Peter and John (v. 14) makes that an impossible task.

Instead, they go into executive session to devise an alternative strategy. It's easier said than done, though, for nobody can think of an effective way to deny what has plainly happened and been seen by so many people (vv. 15-16). Finally, the council comes up with a plan, but, as Amos can attest, it's hardly original: "Let us warn them to speak no more to anyone in this name" (vv. 17-18).

The two apostles respond in a manner reminiscent of Amos. "Whether it is right in God's sight to listen to you rather than to God, you must judge," they declare, "for we cannot keep from speaking about what we have seen and heard" (vv. 19-20). Like Amos before them, Peter and John insist that they are simply being obedient to what God has called them to do, nothing more and nothing less. In other words, the apostles say, "It's not about us." If the council has a problem with this, then the council needs to take the issue up with God, who called them to preach and heal in the first place. Faced with such stubborn obedience, the council has little choice but to let the apostles go (v. 21).

Further analysis shows who the real leaders are. The official leaders have "nothing to say," as contrasted with the "boldness of Peter and John" (vv. 13-14). The whole scene reinforces the believing reader's confidence in the authority of Jesus, in whose name one is saved, for in the silence of the official leadership is fulfilled Jesus' prophecy that his followers' adversaries would be not able to respond to their testimony (Lk 21:15). The official leaders show their lack of integrity in that they do not question "the facts of the case"; they acknowledge that the man was healed, and they cannot deny the reality of what has happened (vv. 15-16). But their only concern is to maintain their position, and this requires that the apostles' message spread no further among "the people." Thus, they command the apostles neither to teach nor speak "in this name" (v. 17). (Chance, 77)

Understanding

Speaking prophetically is dangerous work. It is the kind of calling from which people typically run. Indeed, throughout the

Bible we can find several instances in which God has to overcome the objections of reluctant individuals before they can be used to proclaim God's truth. Consider, for example, the stories of Moses (Ex 3-4), Isaiah (Isa 6), and Jonah (Jon 1), all of whom initially resisted God's call on their lives. We might even say that, by implication, the Bible teaches us to be suspicious of people who eagerly embrace the role of "prophet." Self-serving, self-righteous, and self-proclaimed "prophets" are, unfortunately, never very hard to find.

What makes the brave examples of Amos, Peter, and John so compelling is the utter humility with which they carried out the work that God called them to do. They all made it perfectly clear that they did not speak for themselves. They didn't want to advance any personal agendas, nor did they claim to possess any special eloquence or insight. Instead, they considered themselves servants of God's truth. They acted solely in obedience to God's command.

No doubt it was intimidating for these "uneducated and ordinary men" to stand in the halls of power and speak unpopular and unwelcome truths to people who did not want to hear them, but they knew they did not stand there alone. The God who called them stood alongside them, giving them the courage to say what needed to be said. When we speak up and speak out in pursuit of our own interests and apart from God's will, we stand on far less solid ground.

What About Me?

• *Making people angry is not the same as speaking prophetically.* When sharing God's truth, the substance of what we have to say is obviously of utmost importance. This doesn't mean, however, that style is irrelevant. Insofar as the goal of communication is always to *communicate*, how we say what needs to be said matters a great deal. If our words, tone, or attitude are needlessly provocative or offensive, then those to whom God wants to speak may reject the messenger before they even have a chance to hear the message. Rather, we must speak so that others can hear. At all times—but especially when bearing an unwelcome witness—we do well to remember the Apostle Paul's instruction: Speak the truth in love (Eph 4:15).

• *Dissent is not disloyalty*. People who criticize or question the status quo always risk being labeled as traitors by those with a vested interest in preserving things as they are. The truth is, however, that silence in the face of injustice is the greatest disservice of all. Citizens who love their countries, employees who respect their organizations, and members who care about their churches will brave the potential hostility of others for the sake of moving the world closer to where God wants it to be. Regardless of whether we're *speaking* God's truth or *hearing* God's truth, we must always remember where our true loyalty lies. How we respond to the challenges put before us in these situations will reflect our priorities.

Resources

J. Bradley Chance, *Acts*, Smyth & Helwys Bible Commentary (Macon GA: Smyth & Helwys, 2007).

James Limburg, *Hosea–Micah* (Atlanta: John Knox Press, 1988).

James Meacham, "Q&A: Anglican Bishop N. T. Wright on Resurrection," *The Daily Beast* <http://www.thedailybeast.com/newsweek/2008/04/26/everything-old-is-new-again.html >.

James Nogalski, *The Book of the Twelve: Hosea–Jonah*, Smyth & Helwys Bible Commentary (Macon GA: Smyth & Helwys, 2011).

BOLD WITNESS

Amos 7:10-15; Acts 4:13-22

Troublemakers

When my son Graham was a senior in Fort Worth, he was given the opportunity to introduce one of the honorees at his school's Hall of Fame ceremony. The Paschal High School Hall of Fame is impressive; governors, astronauts, teachers, Olympians, and pastors are among the honored. Actually, by a bizarre oversight there are no pastors, but they do have Dan Jenkins, Charles Tandy, Alan Bean, Liz Smith, and Rebekah Naylor.

That particular year's inductees included the founder of Pancho's Mexican Buffet (which could be considered a somewhat dubious accomplishment), a teacher who worked with learning disabled children, a lawyer who began with the ACLU and ended up producing operas, and a surgeon who was at the Oklahoma City bombing in 1995 who amputated the leg of a woman caught in the rubble and saved her life.

Bill Leonard, the founding dean of Wake Forest's School of Divinity, was also one of the honorees. T Bone Burnett, a musician who has worked with Bob Dylan and Bruce Springsteen, received the most applause when he shouted, "Paschal needs more rock and roll!" Some of the teachers did not seem thrilled with this suggestion.

My son Graham introduced James Dunn, the former executive director of the Baptist Joint Committee on Religious Liberty, who fought courageously for the separation of church and state. Dunn began his speech by saying, "Like Elizabeth Taylor said to each of her eight husbands, I won't keep you long." Most students did not know who Elizabeth Taylor was, but they laughed anyway.

What might have been most interesting was the sense that if you had met the seven people being honored when they were in high school, you probably would not have guessed that they would one day end up in the Hall of Fame. Some were good students, but a few remarked on how they were not. T Bone, in particular, did not spend much time on the honor roll. James Dunn thanked his high school Spanish teacher for teaching him just enough Spanish to keep him out of a jail in Mexico.

Some were outgoing. A few were quiet. They seemed like regular people. But maybe a clue as to what led them to such extraordinary lives could be found in something T Bone said: "It's a scary world, but when I was in high school in 1965 I didn't want to conform to what was considered safe. I couldn't conform. I didn't know how. Don't you conform either. Don't be who they expect you to be. Be who you're supposed to be."

You may have seen the bumper sticker "Well-behaved women seldom make history." Well-behaved men seldom make history either. If biblical heroes like Amos and Simon Peter had gone to Paschal High School, you hope they would be in the Hall of Fame. They might not have been the best students, but they would not conform. They were not who they were expected to be. They lived with amazing courage. They got into trouble.

A Troublemaking Prophet (Am 7:10-15)

Sometimes Amos acted as though he was looking for trouble. He preached threateningly about God's love for the poor. He condemned social inequalities. He announced that King Jeroboam would die and the people would be taken into exile.

Amaziah was the chief priest at the royal chapel who accused Amos of treason. Priests attacking prophets can get ugly. This smackdown takes place at Bethel, where the royal family worshiped. Amaziah's statement, "The land is not able to bear all his words," suggests that the prophet had been causing trouble for a while (v. 10).

Amaziah does not call Amos a false prophet. He does not deny anything Amos said. He just wants the prophet out of his hair. Let him peddle his wares elsewhere, preferably in Judah (v. 12). The priest's argument is not that Amos is wrong, but that he has chosen an inappropriate venue. Amos should refrain from being confrontational when he is at "the king's sanctuary" (v. 13). Propriety is the criterion.

Amos responded to the king's priest, "I am no prophet, nor a prophet's son" (v. 14). The sons of the prophets were groups of prophets who attached themselves to a particular patron. Prophecy had become a profession. Some prophets were on the royal payroll (see 1 Kings 22:6, 10-12). Micah refers to prophets who fit their sermons to the size of their salaries (Mic 3:5). For some, "prophet" had negative connotations (Jer 23:9-22). In this context it is easy to understand why Amos would claim, "I am no prophet."

Amos surprised Amaziah with the news that he was not in it for a paycheck. Amos was not paid to be a minister. He had a job caring for sheep and sycamore trees. Amos told the truth because God told him to tell the truth. The "Go" Amaziah offered is contrasted with the "Go" God spoke (v. 15).

When God speaks to those outside religious institutions, those who benefit from the institutions get upset. Amaziah understands how to get ahead in the religious world. He would be more likely to be invited to speak at a pastors' conference than Amos.

The episode has no real conclusion. This could have been the end of Amos's ministry in the northern kingdom. He might have gone back to Judah. He might have been killed.

We do not know much about what happened to most of the prophets. Isaiah tried to stop being a prophet (Isa 8:16-22). Jeremiah was arrested and then thrown into a well (Jer 36:5, 38:6). Some prophets were killed (Jer 26:20-23).

Preachers are tempted to say what their listeners want to hear. Jesus said, "Woe to you when all speak well of you, for that is what their ancestors did to the false prophets" (Lk 6:26). James Limburg writes,

I recall reading the journal of a well-known theologian and preacher. After hearing a sermon marked by eloquence and soothing charm, he wrote, "Lord, preserve me from eloquence... let my words have a jagged edge." (*Hosea–Micah*, Interpretation [Atlanta: John Knox, 1988] 116)

At their worst, ministers say what will be most welcomed, unlike the heroes and heroines in the Bible, who say whatever jagged word they believe God demands. The truth can be uncomfortable, but God's preachers speak God's word on poverty, peace, and the sins of our leaders.

Troublemaking Preachers (Acts 4:13-22)

God takes quiet people and makes them loud. The Sanhedrin, the seventy most powerful men in Israel, was not sure what to do with Peter and John. The priests and Sadducees, the authorities, and the pillars of the community were annoyed and wanted the new church to follow the rules. The primary desire of most leaders is to preserve the status quo.

This confrontation looks like a mismatch. Peter and John are before the court that condemned Jesus. On one side are the best minds of Judea: the rulers, the elders, the powers that be. On the other side are two uneducated, ordinary men. A pair of fishermen are about to plead their case before the Supreme Court.

Peter and John have to think about how to respond. What would the church want them to do? What is it going to be like at the next business meeting at First Church, Jerusalem? Some will be angry with them for embarrassing the church. If Christians are going to be accepted by mainstream society, then they had to stay out of jail. How could church people be seen as good citizens if Peter and John insisted on getting into trouble?

What would their mothers think? What would you think if it was your son? Peter and John could plea-bargain. They could reassure their captors that they were harmless. What do you think the people at church would want them to do?

The Sanhedrin asks Peter and John, in effect, "What do you think you're doing?" (v. 7). The room gets quiet. Peter and John are not backing down. The Greek word for ordinary in verse 13 is *idiotai*—the root of our word idiot—not a compliment.

This is the same Peter who denied Jesus three times, but he is not going there again. People who know God's grace do not care what the powerful people think. To paraphrase, Peter says, "Rulers, elders, big shots, if our crime is a good deed done to a crippled person, then you need to know that it's God who did it.

You thought you'd killed this movement when you murdered Jesus. You were wrong."

The authorities feel trapped because the religious establishment is supposed to look like it is working for everyone's good. They just want the troublemakers to keep quiet. They retire into executive session (v. 15). They cannot deny the evidence. In an attempt to control the media, the council decides to tell the apostles to keep their mouths shut.

When Peter spoke in chapter 2, 3,000 joined the church. When he delivers the same message to the authorities, no one responds. People who are sure of themselves do not think they need God's help.

Peter and John criticize the council for its inability to lead Israel. These men cannot speak for God because they do not understand God. Peter's call for the council to "judge" is ironic, since they are the ones who should be judged guilty (v. 19).

Peter and John, filled with the audacity and insolence of God's Spirit, reply, "We cannot keep from speaking about what we've seen and heard" (v. 20). They are going to keep doing what they think is right, and if it lands them back in jail, that is fine.

After threatening them again, the Sanhedrin let Peter and John go. The apostles went unpunished not because of the council's devotion to the law, but because the council did not want to anger the people.

Jesus' followers were getting into trouble just as Jesus did. The authorities tried to keep Jesus quiet. Now they tried to keep Peter and John quiet. The opposition gradually built against Jesus, gaining strength against the church. The things that happened to Jesus happen to those who follow Jesus.

Troublemaking Followers

Imagine that one Saturday night your pastor gets a call from the police department. Some people from your church have been arrested for protesting a war at the convention center. When they refused to stop, the police were called. The authorities would like the pastor to help straighten things out. What should the pastor do? Is it the minister's job to advise the troublemakers to calm down? Should Christians get into trouble every now and then?

William Willimon, the former dean of the chapel at Duke University, told an ironic story on himself:

> I grew up in the 60s and like to think of myself as a rabble rouser. But now deep into my 50s, my hair is shorter and so is my vision. I sit among the scribes, rulers, and elders now. Several years ago, a delegation of students came to seek my help in their fight to get Duke University to divest from South Africa. They were polite, well groomed, and wore coats and ties. They said, "We've asked President Sanford to meet with us, but he says he's too busy. We've written him our second letter requesting a conference on this issue, but he hasn't answered yet." I thought to myself, "You little wimps. When I was your age, we wouldn't *ask* the president. We would take over his house, hold his wife hostage, and then tell him what he had to do." Then it hit me. I am the administration. So I told the students to act responsibly. I told them to be patient. I told them that the board knew more than they did. I have learned to cooperate with the powers. (William Willimon, "Trading Places," *The Christian Century* [April 3, 1991] 363)

Christians need to get in trouble. We need to talk about materialism, sexism, pluralism, militarism, evangelism, ecology, homosexuality, and why there are still a couple of places that should not be tattooed. What do we have in common with people like Amos and Peter, who were willing to die rather than deny their faith? What might we be called to do as Christians that might get us in trouble? If we gave ourselves completely to being God's people, what kind of difficulties would we have? Should we be thankful or sad if we seldom get in trouble for our faith?

Notes

Notes

3

POWER CORRUPTS

Daniel 3:8-12, 16-18; Revelation 13:1-10

Central Question

When have I been guilty of idolizing my leader, party, or nation?

Scripture

Daniel 3:8-12, 16-18   8   Accordingly, at this time certain Chaldeans came forward and denounced the Jews. 9 They said to King Nebuchadnezzar, "O king, live forever! 10 You, O king, have made a decree, that everyone who hears the sound of the horn, pipe, lyre, trigon, harp, drum, and entire musical ensemble, shall fall down and worship the golden statue, 11 and whoever does not fall down and worship shall be thrown into a furnace of blazing fire. 12 There are certain Jews whom you have appointed over the affairs of the province of Babylon: Shadrach, Meshach, and Abednego. These pay no heed to you, O King. They do not serve your gods and they do not worship the golden statue that you have set up."... 16 Shadrach, Meshach, and Abednego answered the king, "O Nebuchadnezzar, we have no need to present a defense to you in this matter. 17 If our God whom we serve is able to deliver us from the furnace of blazing fire and out of your hand, O king, let him deliver us. 18 But if not, be it known to you, O king, that we will not serve your gods and we will not worship the golden statue that you have set up."

Revelation 13:1-10 1 And I saw a beast rising out of the sea, having ten horns and seven heads; and on its horns were ten diadems, and on its heads were blasphemous names. 2 And the beast that I saw was like a leopard, its feet were like a bear's, and its mouth was like a lion's mouth. And the dragon gave it his power and his throne and great authority. 3 One of its heads seemed to have received a death-blow, but its mortal wound had been healed. In amazement the whole earth followed the beast. 4 They worshiped the dragon, for he had given his authority to the beast, and they worshiped the beast, saying, "Who is like the beast, and who can fight against it?" 5 The beast was given a mouth uttering haughty and blasphemous words, and it was allowed to exercise authority for forty-two months. 6 It opened its mouth to utter blasphemies against God, blaspheming his name and his dwelling, that is, those who dwell in heaven. 7 Also it was allowed to make war on the saints and to conquer them. It was given authority over every tribe and people and language and nation, 8 and all the inhabitants of the earth will worship it, everyone whose name has not been written from the foundation of the world in the book of life of the Lamb that was slaughtered. 9 Let anyone who has an ear listen: 10 If you are to be taken captive, into captivity you go; if you kill with the sword, with the sword you must be killed. Here is a call for the endurance and faith of the saints.

Reflecting

As Election Day approaches, negative campaign advertisements increasingly pollute the airwaves. Rather than tout their own virtues, political candidates these days often seem to be more interested in ruining the reputations of their opponents. Personal attacks that might once have been considered below-the-belt smear jobs or over-the-top hyperbole now elicit little more than a shrug from people who used to expect more out of our public discourse.

Perhaps most disturbing of all, however, is the degree to which we've become so casual about extreme, inflammatory rhetoric. People who disagree with us aren't simply mistaken—they're Nazis! Leaders whose policies we oppose aren't just misguided—they're traitors! Ideas that we reject aren't merely wrong—they're subversive conspiracies! Exaggerations now routinely roll off our tongues, into one ear and out the other, while comparisons between contemporary leaders and historical evildoers, such as Hitler, Stalin, and Mao, flourish like flies around a compost pile. This kind of rhetorical hyperventilation may be entertaining to some, but it has the effect of trivializing the awful reality of evil in our world. We can only cry "wolf" so many times before people stop listening.

That's why Christians need to be reminded from time to time of what true evil looks like, lest we lose our capacity to recognize it when it surfaces in our midst. Indeed, the Bible tells us that evil can take many forms, corrupting not only individuals, but also institutions intended to serve the common good. Once corrupted, they can then be twisted to serve sinister purposes. In our Scripture readings for today, we see what happens when rulers and governments demand more than they deserve and begin trespassing into holy space that rightfully belongs to God alone. The result is evil, pure and simple—with no room for exaggeration.

Studying

Our Scripture passage from Daniel is a tale of inflated ego and unrestrained power—always a dangerous combination. We're told at the beginning of chapter 3 that King Nebuchadnezzar of Babylon commissioned a gigantic golden statue, roughly ninety feet tall, erected it on the plain of Dura, and then summoned everyone who was anyone in Babylon to gather before the statue and fall to their knees in worship (Dan 3:1-5). This exercise in idolatry was not, of course, entirely voluntary. Conscientious objectors were tossed into a furnace of blazing fire (Dan 3:6).

What prompted Nebuchadnezzar to do such a thing is anybody's guess. The Bible doesn't tell us. One possible explanation is that he did it because he could. Throughout history, this is how tyrants behave. What better way for a king to demonstrate his absolute authority than by commanding a pointless exercise in ritual humiliation? On pain of death, then, the people of Babylon all swallowed their pride and worshiped the ridiculous golden statue (Dan 3:7).

All of them, that is, except Shadrach, Meshach, and Abednego, three Jewish friends who served as royal officials in Babylon. They had come to Babylon as prisoners, taken into exile by Nebuchadnezzar's armies after the conquest of Jerusalem. Though they held important positions in the king's service, they were still strangers in a strange land—and, most importantly, still devoted to the God of Israel. Their exclusive loyalty to God made Nebuchadnezzar's command impossible for them to obey.

News of Shadrach, Meshach, and Abednego's refusal to worship the giant statue soon trickled down to their enemies in the king's court, who pounced on this golden opportunity to denounce them before the king (vv. 8-11). Appealing directly to Nebuchadnezzar's vanity, they described the Jews as brazenly disobedient, arrogant subjects with no regard for the king's words, laws, or gods (v. 12). How dare these foreigners disrespect the great king of Babylon!

For the three friends, however, the great king of Babylon had overstepped his authority. Nebuchadnezzar might be the most powerful man alive, but he had no right to compel his subjects to worship against their will. So Shadrach, Meshach, and Abednego said no—and placed their fate in the hands of the God they served without reservation or compromise. Our God may or may not deliver us from your furnace, they told Nebuchadnezzar, but "be it known to you, O king, that we will not serve your gods and we will not worship the golden statue that you have set up" (v. 18). These three faithful friends knew what was worthy of worship, and, just as importantly, they knew what was not.

A similar dynamic is at work in our other passage for today, which requires some words of introduction. Revelation is an example of apocalyptic literature, which uses rich symbolism of objects, creatures, and numbers to describe the ongoing cosmic struggle between good and evil. Apocalyptic works were usually

written by people suffering under oppressive rulers and, as such, were considered politically dangerous material. This explains the fantastic images and cryptic contents that make apocalyptic literature so distinctive—and hard to interpret. To the original audience, these symbols were familiar and easily deciphered, in much the same way that contemporary readers instantly understand what elephants and donkeys in American political cartoons represent. The vast differences in time and place separating us from first-century Asia Minor, however, wrap a shroud of mystery around Revelation that most of us find intimidating, especially when coming to the book for the first time.

Who was the real-life figure behind "the beast" in Revelation 13? Because New Testament scholars don't know exactly when Revelation was written, they can't be sure who was emperor during the persecution described in the book. One popular candidate for that notorious distinction is the emperor Domitian, who reigned in the late first century and promoted an imperial cult in Asia Minor.

As an apocalyptic work, Revelation was written to encourage and inspire Christians in the midst of persecution (13:10). With that in mind, then, the grotesque scene described in Revelation 13 becomes a little less obscure. The terrible beast (vv. 1-3) represents Rome and its emperors, who claimed divine status and demanded to be worshiped alongside the pagan Roman gods of antiquity (v. 4). Apart from its bizarre appearance, what is distinctive about this beast? Its arrogance (v. 5), its blasphemy (v. 6), and its fierce attacks on the saints (v. 7).

The beast, in other words, has set itself up as a rival of God, demanding the same sort of honor and respect that properly belong to God alone. Accordingly, we're told, the people of the earth will divide themselves into two groups: those who worship the beast and those who remain faithful to God (v. 8). Revelation offers no third option.

Understanding

In a world filled with idols, distinguishing what is worthy of worship from what isn't is an essential spiritual survival skill, for in order to resist evil we must first be able to *recognize* it. In Daniel, evil took the form of a coercive policy mandating the worship of a golden statue. In Revelation, evil took the form of a profane, violent beast that demanded worship while opposing God's will and work. While it's true that in both cases, evil manifested itself through the activities of earthly rulers and governments, this doesn't mean that earthly rulers and governments are, as a rule, inherently evil. On the contrary, the Apostle Paul tells us in Romans 13:1-8 that God instituted civil authority for our benefit, to maintain order, and to punish those who threaten the common good.

Government is not evil in Daniel and Revelation. Idolatry is. Indeed, worshiping anything other than God is wrong—and people, political parties, or governments that encourage, demand, or compel others to practice idolatry do evil in the sight of the Lord. This reality is as old as the first two commandments God gave us in Exodus 20:3-5: "You shall have no other gods before me. You shall not make for yourself an idol.... You shall not bow down to them or worship them." Only God is worthy of our worship.

Recognizing the evil of officially sanctioned idolatry is one thing. Resisting it is quite another. As God's faithful people in an unfaithful world, we are called to resist evil, but such resistance comes at a high price, as both of our Scripture passages indicate.

> A church member commented, "I give as much of my time to the church as I do to my political party." How would you respond to that statement?

Whether it's the fiery furnaces of Babylon or the iron might of Rome, the rebellious powers of this world have ways of forcing knees to bend and heads to bow in the wrong direction. We can be encouraged that God wins in the end, but between now and then there may be trials to endure and, when it comes to resisting evil, moments when we will have to learn how to say no if we are to preserve the integrity of our faith.

What About Me?

• *Keep things in perspective.* Lots of folks complain about mean-spirited, extreme political rhetoric, but few people ever dare to stand up against the verbal bullies who often dominate our public conversations. Christians can—and should—do better than that. In fact, we can—and should—set examples of how to express political opinions in a responsible, informed fashion. This means resisting the temptation to use inflammatory words such as "evil" to describe those with whom we simply disagree regarding the issues of the day. The Bible tells us clearly what true evil looks like, so let's not indulge in reckless exaggeration for the sake of scoring points in an argument. Not only is it unnecessary, but it also displays an ignorance of the biblical witness that is unbecoming of a disciple of Christ.

• *Beware of idols in disguise.* Idolatry has become much more subtle since the days of Nebuchadnezzar's golden statue and Rome's decadent emperors, but it certainly has not disappeared. Flags, political parties, leaders, and even nations themselves can become focal points for devotion in ways that undermine our whole-hearted commitment to God. Where does our ultimate trust lie? To whose work do we make our largest financial contributions? Whose values primarily shape our decisions? To whom do we turn first for guidance? Whose symbols decorate our places of worship? If the answer to any of these questions is something (or someone) other than God, then we may already be practicing idolatry without even knowing it, which is, by far, the most dangerous kind of idolatry.

Resources

Sharon Pace, *Daniel*, Smyth & Helwys Bible Commentary (Macon GA: Smyth & Helwys, 2008).

Mitchell G. Reddish, *Revelation*, Smyth & Helwys Bible Commentary (Macon GA: Smyth & Helwys, 2001).

POWER CORRUPTS

Daniel 3:8-12, 16-18; Revelation 13:1-10

What the Authorities Teach

I grew up in the segregated South. The authorities taught me to leave things alone. We sang "red and yellow, black and white, they are precious in his sight," but we did not mean three quarters of it. Rosalyn Carter once said this of a politician for whom she did not care, "He made us comfortable with our prejudice." The politicians in Mississippi were comfortable teaching me to keep my distance from African Americans long before the Carter years.

The authorities taught me that God was on their side. Our leaders quoted from the King James Version of the Bible, but none of the verses they referenced had to do with our responsibility to feed the hungry or welcome the outsider. They claimed the Bible as their authority, but we were not encouraged to read it for ourselves. Maybe those in power were afraid of what we would find if we did.

The people in power made it clear that questioning the Vietnam War made you questionable. The worst of our leaders work to convince people that the authorities need more power. The United States has amassed the most formidable weapons systems the world has seen. Our military spending is equal to that of the rest of the world put together. The combined military budgets of Iran, North Korea, Cuba, and Syria are less than four percent of our budget. We have delivery systems capable of reaching any spot on earth. Should it trouble Christians that a U.S. nuclear submarine capable of terrible destruction is named *Corpus Christi,* "the body of Christ"?

Some politicians deceive good citizens into voting for them with disingenuous promises. I have had conversations with homeless people about addiction, AIDS, and abuse, but the most painful conversations are about politics. Some who desperately need treatment for mental illness back politicians who are against health care. Some single mothers with malnourished children think the greatest threat to their children comes from those who work for peace. Some of the unemployed support politicians who are against job training. They have been hoodwinked into supporting the powers that be without question. Christians should not fall in line with those with the most money and power. We should guard against the tendency to idolize government leaders—no matter who is in power.

The Abuse of Power (Dan 3:8-12; 16-18)

Daniel 3 describes a conflict between the powerful and the faithful. Nebuchadnezzar commanded his subjects to worship a golden image. The Greek version of Daniel indicates that the statue went up the year Babylon conquered Jerusalem.

Shadrach, Meshach, and Abednego had been made officials in Babylon at Daniel's request. Daniel is then oddly absent from chapter 3. Many commentators see this as evidence that this story was originally independent from the Daniel stories. "Chaldeans" came forward and denounced the three Jews for not worshiping the idol. The use of the term Chaldeans for Babylonians may be intended to be ethnically specific. The Jews' real crime is being foreigners who have been given authority.

The groveling before King Nebuchadnezzar is humorous. The music plays and the people fall down. The instruments listed—horn, pipe, lyre, trigon, harp, and drum—would make quite a squeaky orchestra.

The text does not say that the statue is Nebuchadnezzar, but the king acts like an arrogant tyrant. The Babylonians used fire as a punishment in other instances (see Jer 29:22). The king throws down the gauntlet directly at God: "Who is the god that will deliver you out of my hands?" (Dan 3:15). Shadrach, Meshach, and Abednego answer the king with a plea of *nollo contendere*, "O Nebuchadnezzar, we have no need to present a defense to you" (v. 16).

If God delivers them, then so be it. But if God does not, they still won't worship the golden image. The reaction of the accused is to declare their independence from the government. This is civil disobedience at its best. They are not sure that God will deliver them, but they are sure of what they must do. In their statement of loyalty to God, even in the worst case, these three have already defeated the government. The most infuriating aspect of radical faith is the refusal to bow before the powers that be.

This story may remind us of the stories of Joseph and Esther. A conspiracy threatens the hero. When things are at their most frightening, the hero's greatness is recognized. He or she is given an even higher standing than before.

Daniel 3 is a call not to lose heart before the powers. The king demanded a loyalty oath and the heroes refused. John Calvin loved this scene, "When therefore, death was placed straight before their eyes, they did not turn aside from the straightforward course, but treated God's glory of greater value than their own life, nay than a hundred lives, if they had so many to prove faith" (W. Sibley Towner, *Daniel*, Interpretation [Atlanta: John Knox, 1985] 51). The early Christians refused military service because of Jesus' commands to love one's enemies. People of faith have a loyalty that supersedes any government.

Absolute Power (Rev 13:1-10)

Nebuchadnezzar in Daniel 3 and the beast in Revelation 13 were not evil because they espoused policy positions with which people disagreed. They were evil because they demanded complete loyalty. Revelation 12 ends with the dragon standing on the seashore. Then another beast rises out of the sea (13:1). This beast has ten horns, seven heads, and ten crowns. The beast is like a leopard with the feet of a bear and the mouth of a lion. Three of the beasts in the book of Daniel are merged into one (Dan 7:4-6).

The dragon transferred its power to the beast (Rev 13:2). One of the beast's heads recovered from a wound and people were astonished. In the face of the dragon's awesome power, the whole world follows. Their amazement—"Who is like the beast, and who can fight against it?" (13:4)—is a combination of awe at the beast's military power and despair (Christopher Rowland,

"Revelation," *New Interpreter's Bible Commentary* [Nashville TN: Abingdon, 1998] 657).

The beast is reminiscent of the fourth beast in Daniel 7:8, 11, and 20. The beast blasphemes not only the name of God but also God's dwelling (Rev 13:6)— the heavenly temple. Forty-two months (three and a half years) is a symbolic period of end-times distress (Dan 7:25).

John is confronting emperor worship. When he wrote Revelation, Christianity was the religion of a tiny minority persecuted by the state. John holds out no false hope of rescue from death for those who remain faithful (Rev 13:7). The divine mystery is a Lamb who was slain, a victim of the powers, yet faithful and true. The criterion for inclusion in the book of life is to resist worshiping the beast.

The beast represents the power of evil that attracts admiration for its military strength. People are easily deceived by power. Hitler, Stalin, and Pol Pot could not have committed their horrible crimes without the support of ordinary people, including many Christians who tried only to avoid being seen as political.

Most Christians make accommodation to the state. Revelation calls us to ask hard questions about uncritical cooperation with the powers. Neutrality is the tool of the status quo. The church was never meant to be cautious. The church should challenge.

Standing Up to the Powers

Christians have no business idolizing any leader, party, or nation. "My country, right or wrong" makes no sense to a person of faith. Our good country could do better. We could do a better job of caring for the poor. Faith is feeding the hungry, watching out for the disadvantaged, and standing up for the people who are losing. The way we respond to poverty is a litmus test for courage. Jim Wallis often says, "We have to oppose a government of the wealthy, by the wealthy, and for the wealthy."

Christians need to oppose leaders and systems that ignore the needs of children. The Hebrew prophets said that how we treat orphans is the measure of our love for God. Jesus said that those who cause harm to a child would be better off thrown into the sea with millstones around their necks. The disciples tried to push children to the back of the line, but Jesus made it clear that children need to be moved to the front. For Christians, our response to children reveals the level of our commitment to the one who said, "Whoever welcomes one such child in my name welcomes me" (Mt 18:5). God's people work for a just society that benefits every child.

Courageous Christians wage peace. We should be concerned about the cost of war, the present wars, the next war, the shedding of blood, the wasting of innocent life, the demeaning of people, the destruction of property, the poverty, and the hatred. Peacemaking is central to the life of faith. Scripture commands us to "seek peace, and pursue it" (Ps 34:14). Jesus blessed "the peacemakers" (Mt 5:9). Jesus is pro-peace. Would the one who commanded us to love our enemies think we do enough to avoid war? Leaders try to appear unyielding, afraid that any sign of concern will be interpreted as weakness. They promise not to negotiate, as though listening could be a mistake. When war is portrayed as the less painful option, we need to speak the hope of peace. Killing terrorists will not defeat terrorism. Pre-emptive wars will not make us safer. Crushing a few despots can perpetuate hatred. It is clear that war on Islamic countries will ultimately increase the number of Islamic terrorists. If the United States supported a policy based more on human rights, international law, and sustainable development for poor countries, and less on arms transfers and military attacks, we would all be safer.

Our national security has to be based on more than military power. We should push for diplomacy, economic development, and the protection of human rights. We should recognize that poverty and national humiliation are as dangerous to our security as any weapon. We need to return to the most effective ways America has influenced nations throughout the world, by offering a helping hand and abiding by our deepest principles. Ours is an amazing country with lofty, worthy goals. Brave Christians work to make our nation more just.

In *Ah! But Your Land is Beautiful* (London: Penguin, 1983), Alan Paton tells the story of Robert Mansfield, a white man in South Africa thirty years ago. Mansfield was the headmaster of a white school who took his athletic teams to play cricket against the black schools. When the department of education forbade him to do it anymore, he resigned in protest. Shortly thereafter, Emmanuel Nene, a leader in the black community, came to meet him.

"I have come to see a man who resigns his job, because he doesn't wish to obey an order that will prevent children from playing with one another."

"Mr. Nene, I resigned because I think it is time to go out and fight everything that separates people from one another. Do I look like a knight in shining armor?"

"Yes, you do, but you're going to get wounded. Do you know that?"

"I expect that may happen."

"Well you expect correctly, Mr. Mansfield. People don't like what you're doing. But I am thinking of joining with you in the battle."

"You're going to wear the shining armor, too."

"Yes, and I'm going to get wounded, too. Not only by the government, but also by my own people as well."

"Aren't you worried about the wounds, Mr. Nene?"

"I don't worry about the wounds. When I go up there, which is my intention, the Big Judge will say to me, 'Where are your wounds?' and if I say 'I haven't any,' he will say, 'Was there nothing to fight for?' I couldn't face that question."

You and I will stand before God and hear the question, "Where are your wounds? Was there no prejudice left to battle? Were there no frightened people who needed your help? Were there no homeless families, unemployed veterans, or poor children? Were there no wars that should have been stopped? Where are your scars?"

Notes

Notes

4

PRAYER FOR RULERS

Psalm 72:1-7; 1 Timothy 2:1-4

Central Question

How should I pray for the leaders of my community, state, and country?

Scripture

Psalm 72:1-7 1 Give the king your justice, O God, and your righteousness to a king's son. 2 May he judge your people with righteousness, and your poor with justice. 3 May the mountains yield prosperity for the people, and the hills, in righteousness. 4 May he defend the cause of the poor of the people, give deliverance to the needy, and crush the oppressor. 5 May he live while the sun endures, and as long as the moon, throughout all generations. 6 May he be like rain that falls on the mown grass, like showers that water the earth. 7 In his days may righteousness flourish and peace abound, until the moon is no more.

1 Timothy 2:1-4 1 First of all, then, I urge that supplications, prayers, intercessions, and thanksgivings be made for everyone, 2 for kings and all who are in high positions, so that we may lead a quiet and peaceable life in all godliness and dignity. 3 This is right and is acceptable in the sight of God our Savior, 4 who desires everyone to be saved and to come to the knowledge of the truth.

Reflecting

As part of its standard liturgy, the Episcopalian *Book of Common Prayer* includes prayers for those who hold positions of worldly authority. These prayers are included not because of who they are or what parties and policies they represent, but rather because of the heavy responsibilities that come with these positions of public leadership.

Governing well, wisely, and in support of the common good is not an easy task. In order to fulfill their obligations to the best of their ability, public servants need all the help they can get. Praying for our elected and appointed leaders is one way Christians can support those who are working on our behalf.

Praying for our leaders is not only a prudent exercise (our leaders are more likely to make good decisions if they are being guided by the Holy Spirit) but it's a biblical practice as well. In both the Old and New Testaments, God's people are instructed to pray for their leaders.

Admittedly, it can be a challenge to pray for men and women for whom we didn't vote and with whose ideas we don't agree. The Bible, however, doesn't make any partisan distinctions. In fact, the Apostle Paul tells the Christians in Rome that they should consider the civil authority "God's servant for your good" (Rom 13:4). As such, those in authority, regardless of whether they are Republicans, Democrats, independents, liberals, or conservatives, are worthy of our prayers.

What is the best way, though, for us to pray for our leaders? Today's Scripture passages from Psalm 72 and 1 Timothy 2:1-4 offer some constructive advice. The bottom line, however, is that good leaders make good decisions, which benefits everybody in the long run. As prayers go, that's a good place to start!

Studying

Our passage from Psalm 72 was most likely meant to be sung as part of a royal coronation ceremony for a new Davidic king. In much the same way that presidential inaugurations in the United States are usually occasions of great pomp, circumstance, and optimism, the elevation of a new king to rule over God's people was a time for rejoicing and looking forward with hope. A spirit of joyful goodwill permeates this psalm, so much so that it effectively serves as a public prayer for the new king. Do you want a biblical example of how to pray for those in positions of civil authority? Then look no further than Psalm 72.

First and foremost, the psalmist prays that the new king will rule not with just *any* kind of justice and righteousness, but specifically with *God's* justice and *God's* righteousness (v. 1). Behind these words, of course, lies years of history between God and God's people, an ongoing relationship in which, time and again, God demonstrated great patience, compassion, and generosity to a rebellious nation that rarely deserved such kindness. To be just as God is just and righteous as God is righteous are tall orders for a new king. Yet these are the first blessings for which the psalmist prays, suggesting that justice and righteousness are indeed the necessary cornerstones upon which good leadership must rest.

The psalmist then expresses great hope for what that good leadership will look like in practice. The prayer reads like a wish list. What does a good king do? He makes decisions based on what's right and not on who's rich (v. 2). He works to bring prosperity to all the people, not just a few (v. 3). He is particularly careful to defend the weak and vulnerable against those who would take advantage of them (v. 4). His policies generate widespread growth in the same way that rain indiscriminately waters the earth (v. 6). His rule is marked by integrity and peace, presumably not only within the kingdom of Judah itself, but also between the kingdom and its neighbors as well (v. 7).

While the psalmist prays for a new king about to begin his reign, the Apostle Paul instructs his young friend Timothy (and presumably those Christians under Timothy's pastoral care) to lift up those who already exercise authority over God's people. Paul is not content to urge "prayers," simply and generically. Rather, he uses four different words— supplications, prayers, intercessions, and thanksgivings (1 Tim 2:1)—to indicate the many facets of human-divine communication that believers should engage in for the sake of their leaders. Gloer explains the nuances of these various terms:

> It seems clear that "prayers" is the generic term for prayer, while the other three terms express various elements that are to be included in prayer. "Supplications" (*deeseis*) refers to asking with urgency based on personal need. "Intercessions" (*enteuxeis*; found only here and in 4:15 in the New Testament) suggests the importance of praying for others. "Thanksgivings"(*eucharistias*) refers to expressing gratitude for blessings or benefits. Paul's intention here is not to set one type of prayer over against another. Neither is it to limit prayer to these elements alone. His desire is to encourage Christians to be faithful in prayer. (137)

In other words, Christians must not be stingy in their prayerful support of "kings and all who are in high positions" (v. 2). Because the responsibilities of these leaders are great, so is their need for divine guidance. Furthermore, Paul urges these prayers to "be made for everyone" (v. 1). The prayers of believers are to be as unlimited as the grace of God (Gloer, 138).

In directing Timothy to pray, however, Paul cites another, more mundane, but no less compelling, reason to commend our leaders to God's mercy and direction. Pray for those in authority, Paul writes, "so that we may lead a quiet and peaceable life in all godliness and dignity" (v. 2). Given the tenuous circumstances of Christians in the Roman Empire—those of a small, powerless minority subject to sporadic outbursts of persecution—Paul's rationale is well grounded.

Understandably, neither Paul, nor Timothy, nor any other Christian wished to attract negative attention from the emperor or his underlings. Indeed, the immediate physical and economic security of Christians in the empire depended almost entirely upon the goodwill—or at the very least, the benign neglect, of the civil authorities. So for Paul, it made perfect sense for Christians to pray specifically that their leaders would see fit to leave them alone to live quietly, peacefully, and in obedience to Jesus Christ.

Paul's expectations for worldly government were much more modest than those of the psalmist. The latter prayed that with God's guidance and inspiration, Israel's king would rule as

God would rule: generously, justly, and righteously. Psalm 72 provides an expansive, hopeful vision of what worldly power can accomplish.

For Paul, however, a government that simply maintained public order and protected the basic rights of minorities (two tasks which are, admittedly, not always easy to do) would be the answer to a prayer. His vision is more limited, but in its own way, perhaps no less hopeful than the psalmist's.

Indeed, Paul understood that a government that allowed Christians to live "in all godliness and dignity" (v. 2) would unwittingly further the will of God, "who desires everyone to be saved and to come to the knowledge of the truth" (v. 4). After all, Christians who are free to live out their faith are Christians who are free to *share* their faith, and that kind of freedom, Paul believes, is definitely worth praying for!

Understanding

Times change. Circumstances change. Forms of government change. These changes can complicate our efforts to take lessons from the past and apply them to the present. It's no surprise that the psalmist, writing in Judah under a divinely sanctioned monarchy, and the Apostle Paul, writing as a member of a sometimes-persecuted minority under the rule of a pagan emperor, differ in their understandings of and expectations for civil authority. Likewise, the perspectives of readers living in a twenty-first century Western democracy will be shaped by their own experience of how worldly power is exercised. These

> Let every person be subject to the governing authorities; for there is no authority except from God, and those authorities that exist have been instituted by God. (Rom 13:1)

> Honor everyone. Love the family of believers. Fear God. Honor the emperor. (1 Pet 2:17)

> Paul said, "I am appealing to the emperor's tribunal; this is where I should be tried. I have done no wrong to the Jews, as you very well know. Now if I am in the wrong and have committed something for which I deserve to die, I am not trying to escape death; but if there is nothing to their charges against me, no one can turn me over to them. I appeal to the emperor." (Acts 25:10-11)

ever-changing realities mean that connecting the dots between different eras is, at best, an imprecise operation.

It is not, however, an impossible one. Indeed, while neither the psalmist nor Paul wrote in a context of representative democracy and the separation of church and state, they both agree on a central principle that transcends time and place: God's people ought to pray for their leaders.

This is not a "partisan" issue. Praying for our elected officials doesn't mean that we agree with everything they say and do. Surely Paul did not agree with everything said or done in the name of Nero, who viciously persecuted Christians and was emperor when scholars believe Paul was martyred in Rome. One might even say that the fact that worldly powers sometimes act contrary to the will of God gives even greater incentive for Christians to pray for them.

We should not pray for our leaders only when we like them nor withhold our prayers when they embrace policies we oppose. Instead, taking our cue both from the psalmist and from Paul, we should pray for our elected and appointed public servants since if they do their jobs well and faithfully meet the obligations that come with their positions, then the common good will be served and everyone will benefit. In any era, under any government, this biblical principle stands the test of time.

How do you pray for your favorite sports team when they are in the midst of a difficult game? How is this like or unlike the way you pray for elections or for elected officials? How do our prayers for public officials reflect our faith that God can handle difficult situations without the help of capable leaders?

What About Me?

• *How should I pray for my leaders?* Psalm 72 provides a good model for us to follow. In it, the psalmist asks God to help the king rule with justice and righteousness. As governing virtues go, these are perhaps the most essential. Indeed, without a basic sense of what is just and right, leaders have little hope of making wise decisions. At the very least, then, prayers for those who exercise worldly power should begin by asking God to help them lead justly and righteously. Beyond that, we can let our conscience be our guide.

• *What does it mean to pray for leaders with whom I disagree?* It means that we are practicing forbearance, a Christian virtue closely related to patience. We may vehemently oppose the policies our leaders implement. At any given moment, roughly half the country will probably feel that way. The virtue of forbearance, which is sometimes translated as "gentleness" in the New Testament (see, for example, Eph 4:2), in no way implies agreement, but rather, just the opposite. Forbearance involves the determination to wait patiently and prayerfully while God changes enemies into friends. Forbearance not only requires trust, it requires humility. After all, it may turn out that, in God's time, we are the ones who need to change!

• *When should I start praying for my leaders?* Today! The prayers of Christians seeking God's guidance for their leaders are always in season, but with a major election rapidly approaching, now is an especially important time to be about this good work. And when all the votes have been counted? Our *leaders* may change, but our prayers do not. May God grant those who hold positions of civil authority the wisdom to rule with justice and righteousness and in pursuit of the common good.

Resources

W. Hulitt Gloer, *1 & 2 Timothy–Titus*, Smyth & Helwys Bible Commentary (Macon GA: Smyth & Helwys, 2010).

The Book of Common Prayer (New York: Seabury, 1979).

PRAYER FOR RULERS

Psalm 72:1-7; 1 Timothy 2:1-4

Reasons to Give Thanks

A few summers ago, Carol and I were in Washington DC. We went to the National Archives, where even standing in line is inspiring. The original Declaration of Independence, 1776, is on the left: "We hold these truths to be self-evident, that all men are created equal, that they are endowed by their creator with certain inalienable rights, among these are life, liberty and the pursuit of happiness." That declaration was a torch that lit up the whole world. No one had ever said in such a glorious way that people have a right to rule themselves. The rich and poor should have equal standing. We forget how stunning it was.

The Constitution, in the center, is the longest lasting written constitution in the world. The Founding Fathers rejected the idea of property qualifications for holding office because they wanted no part of "veneration for wealth." Their goal was to preserve equal opportunities by destroying any alliance between government and money.

The Bill of Rights may be even more amazing. The first amendment reads, "Congress shall make no law respecting an establishment of religion, or prohibiting the free exercise thereof; or abridging the freedom of speech, or of the press." That amendment puts every citizen on the same footing. It made us a beacon of freedom to the rest of the world.

Carol and I were following a father and daughter around the rotunda. We heard the father whisper, "This is the Bill of Rights. It says that every person is free."

The little girl stared at the aging, fading document and said, "It looks like it's falling apart."

To which her father replied, "It's been through a lot."

We went to the Lincoln Memorial, where the Gettysburg Address is on Lincoln's right: "That this nation under God, shall have a new birth of freedom—and that government of the people, by the people, for the people shall not perish from the earth." Lincoln's second inaugural address—delivered a little over a month before his assassination in 1865—is on the wall to Lincoln's left:

> Neither party expected for the war the magnitude or the duration which it has already attained. Both read the same Bible and pray to the same God, and each invokes His aid against the other. It may seem strange that any men should dare to ask a just God's assistance in wringing their bread from the sweat of other men's faces, but let us judge not, that we be not judged. The prayers of both could not be answered.

When we went to the World War II Memorial, I spoke with a lady from New York. She brought her grandson, because she wanted him to understand. She played the violin in the navy orchestra and sorted military mail. She said, "It was a horrible war. Too many people on both sides died." The World War II Memorial was like a reunion. The crowd was laughing and smiling. There were uniforms, medals, walkers, wheelchairs, and old friends hugging. A group of African-American veterans all wore the same baseball caps.

The atmosphere at the Vietnam Memorial was different. The monument includes the names of 58,000 soldiers who died from 1959–1975. Each name was followed by a diamond or a cross. The diamond indicates that the individual's death was confirmed. The 1,100 names followed by a cross were either missing or prisoners at the end of the war. If a person returns alive a circle is to be inscribed around the cross, but I did not see any circles. The crowd was different than the one at the World War II Memorial. There were sixty-year-old women who I imagined were widows. Forty-year-olds were looking for their fathers' names.

At the FDR Memorial there is a quotation that makes Roosevelt sound like a prophet: "Unless the peace that follows recognizes that the whole world is one neighborhood and does justice to the whole human race, the germs of another world war will remain as a constant threat to mankind."

Praying for the King (Ps 72:1-7)

The nation of Israel longed for peace. Their part of the world was trampled in war after war. Peace seemed impossible. They sang songs to David and Solomon because their other kings make Richard Nixon look like Abraham Lincoln. Justice was for sale and most did not have enough for a down payment. Children were starving while selfish tyrants were eating their fill every night. The bad guys were winning. The good guys were losing hope. Even though they were close to giving in to despair, they came to worship and sang this prayer for a king who would make it all right.

Psalm 72 is a poem composed for the inauguration of a Davidic king in Jerusalem. The psalm was not about any particular king, so it could be used repeatedly. The prayer is that God will bring about God's rule on earth. Many believed that power flowed from God to the people through the kings. The title "Of Solomon" suggests another way of understanding the psalm. The scribe may have seen connections to the account of Solomon choosing to pray for wisdom to judge his people with justice (1 Kings 3:3-14).

The opening petition asks for a great gift for a king, the judgments and righteousness of God (v. 1). Verses 2-7 describe *shalom*, peace—which is primarily concerned with care for the poor. The only stated responsibility of the king is to establish justice for the hurting: "May he defend the cause of the poor of the people, give deliverance to the needy, and crush the oppressor" (v. 4). The people pray that the king will outlive the sun and the moon (v. 5).

Psalm 72 functioned both as a charge to and a prayer for the new king, but the kings of Israel and Judah did not behave much like the king described in the poem. Even after the final failure of the monarchy, the psalm continued to be read as a proclamation of God's hopes. By the time it became part of the Psalter, it was almost certainly understood as a prayer for the coming Messiah (James Luther Mays, *Psalms*, Interpretation [Louisville KY: John Knox, 1994] 238).

For Christians, Jesus fulfilled the vision. When Christians pray, "Thy kingdom come, thy will be done, on earth as it is in heaven," they are praying this psalm (J. Clinton McCann Jr., "Psalms," *New Interpreter's Bible Commentary* [Nashville TN: Abingdon, 1996] 965).

Psalm 72 reminds us that we find the way to peace when power works for justice. Many Christians neglect to pray for politicians, but we need to pray for them because we want God to help them. We need to pray that our leaders "defend the cause of the poor of the people" (v. 4).

Praying for Our Government (1 Tim 2:1-4)

The author of 1 Timothy says prayers should be made for all. The writer puts together near synonyms—"supplication, prayers, intercessions, and thanksgivings" (v. 1). The people should pray "for kings and all who are in high positions." They are to pray to "lead a quiet and peaceable life in all godliness and dignity" (v. 2).

One way to read verse 2 is as a result of the desire for acceptance. Being seen as loyal to the state can be politically helpful, but it can also mean accommodation to the culture. Their desire for a "quiet and peaceable life" is in tension with the way the church in Acts turned the world upside-down. The wish for "godliness and dignity" might seem like a longing for respectability that avoids controversy.

We must remember that the position of the early Christians was precarious. Although they were not yet persecuted for their faith, people looked on them with suspicion. Any hint of rebelliousness might lead to trouble, which might be why the author suggests that prayers be made for "kings and all who are in high positions."

God wants everyone to be saved (v. 4). Kings and lesser government officials are themselves recipients of God's favor. God's hope is that everyone know the truth. Most Christians do not make a habit of praying for government leaders, but we should.

Praying for Our Country

How should we pray for our leaders? Americans have chosen sides and stopped being kind to those on the other team. This is not what the writers of Psalm 72 and 1 Timothy had in mind. We are to pray that our leaders will be concerned for the poor because we all benefit from a caring government.

The United States has a history of welcoming tired, poor, huddled masses. We led the world in providing schools for children and care for the elderly. We made great progress in giving justice to all. Our country has, in many ways, lived out the goodness of her core values. We have been blessed and been a blessing, but we are tempted to hoard what we have been given.

Some of the greatest patriots point out how our country is not all it can be. Like the prophet Micah, they call us to do justice. Like Peter, they say, "We must obey God rather than any human authority." We always have room to improve because government too easily falls into the hands of those who favor the haves over the have-nots.

The gap between rich and poor in the United States is greater than it has been in fifty years. Poverty is showing up where we have not expected it: among families that include two parents who work. Some of these newly poor love their children, go to church, and work hard all week, but although they are running hard, they keep falling farther behind. The gap between them and prosperous America is widening and hardening. Hard-working people who became accustomed to putting in longer hours just to stay in place are now losing their jobs. Meanwhile, the Republicans and Democrats argue over who is the real champion of the middle class. Most politicians do not seem to care about those with the greatest needs.

Christians of good will can disagree about the role of government and what policies best serve the cause of justice for all. There is room for debate about such things, but if we are following Christ we cannot disagree about our responsibility to care for the hurting. Jesus lived with compassion for the poor and forgotten. Christ's followers live with the same compassion. God wants to bless America by making our country more caring. We raise our voices for those who do not get heard. We work for affordable housing, job opportunities, care for the sick, and possibilities for the working poor.

We ask hard questions about our government's policies. Do they represent the common good of society or the interest of an elite few? Do they show sensitivity to the spirit of the Golden Rule? Do they refrain from the arrogant assumption that the powerful have the right to ignore the needs of the hurting? Do they widen the gap between rich and poor? What would God have us do?

God inspired a Methodist ship worker named Edward Rogers to crusade across New England for an eight-hour work day. God inspired a young priest named John Ryan to champion child labor laws, unemployment insurance, a minimum wage, and decent housing for the poor ten years before the New Deal. God inspired Dorothy Day to challenge the church to march alongside auto workers in Michigan. God inspired E. B. McKinney to challenge a system in Mississippi that kept sharecroppers in servitude and debt. God inspired a Presbyterian minister named Eugene Carson Blake—"Ike's Pastor"—who was arrested for protesting racial injustice in Baltimore. God inspired Martin Luther King Jr. to go to Memphis to join sanitation workers in their struggle for a decent wage (Bill Moyers, "Call to Renewal Keynote Address," Washington DC, 24 May 2004).

Caring for the disadvantaged, the hurting, and the poor is not a partisan issue. It does not matter if you are a liberal or a conservative, Jesus is both and neither. It does not matter if you are a Democrat or a Republican—Jesus is both and neither. God calls us to become more like Christ by caring for the hurting. God wants us to pray that our leaders will love more like God does.

Notes

Notes

nextsunday
STUDIES

1 Peter
Keep Hope Alive

This study of First Peter focuses on keeping hope alive in the face of pressures and circumstances that could possibly extinguish it completely, or worse, turn authentic faith into a pale replica of the real thing.

Advent Virtues

The phrase "holiday rush" is not an exaggeration. The frantic pace required to purchase gifts, bake holiday foods, and attend Christmas parties, plays, and performances takes its toll; we arrive at Christmas Day exhausted. Within the context of December busyness, the ancient Christian season of Advent takes on new meaning and acquires renewed importance. May God instill the virtues of *hope*, *peace*, *joy*, *love*, and *faith* in each of us this Advent.

Apocalyptic Literature

This study examines five apocalyptic texts in the Bible—from Zechariah, Daniel, Matthew, and Revelation. With each new year bringing a new prediction of impending doom, it is always a perfect time to get the story straight. Apocalyptic literature does not address the future. It addresses our present.

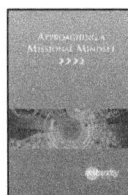

Approaching a Missional Mindset

The World isn't the same as it once was. We must be the church in a new place, in unimagined ways, and with a wider range of people. Engage your small group with the radical and refreshing challenge of developing a "missional lifestyle."

Baptist Freedom
Celebrating Our Baptist Heritage

What makes a Baptist a Baptist? Of course, the ultimate answer is simple: membership in a local Baptist church. But there are all kinds of Baptist churches! What are the spiritual and theological marks of a Baptist? What is the shape and the feel of Baptist Christianity?

The Bible and the Arts

God has used artistic expression throughout the centuries to convey truth, offer blessing, and urge believers to deeper faithfulness. In modern life, artistic expression flourishes, from movies to books to music to paintings to photographs. Sometimes artists are intentional about trying to portray God's truths. Other times, perhaps God is working even when the artist is unaware of it. As believers, we may hear and see God at work in many art forms.

The Birthday of a King

The first four lessons in this unit draw inspiration from a traditional interpretation of the Advent candles as the Prophets' Candle, the Bethlehem Candle, the Shepherds' Candle, and the Angels' Candle. The final lesson, which occurs after Advent, celebrates the theological meaning of Jesus' birth as described in the prologue to John's Gospel.

Challenges of the Christian Life

The way of the cross is difficult, and taking Jesus seriously means looking honestly at how we fall short of God's best hopes for us and seeing how much we need God's grace. For all of us there are times when we need to remember that Christ is our saving grace and recommit ourselves to the journey of faith, rediscovering, again and again, the life-giving purpose described in the book of Ephesians.

Christ Is Born!

Even in the midst of difficult circumstances, Advent is a time when we can find hope. Much like today, people in the 1st century church faced struggles. Examining the Gospel of Matthew, lessons include "Waiting for Christ," "Preparing for Christ," "Expecting Christ," "Announcing Christ," and "The Arrival of Christ."

Christians and Hunger

These sessions challenge us to apply gospel lenses and holy imagination to what literally gives us energy to live: food. With God's grace, we have the opportunity to imagine communities where tables are large and all are fed.

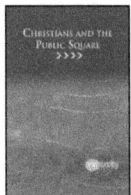

Christians and the Public Square

Politics and faith are tricky areas for Christians to negotiate. The First Amendment to the Constitution guarantees religious freedom for all Americans. As Christians who are also citizens, questions abound: How do we distinguish between faithful and unfaithful forms of civic engagement? How do we give Caesar his due while giving our all to God?

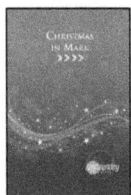

Christmas in Mark

In the early chapters of Mark, we will encounter a Christmas story. This story, however, will not be quite like the one told by other Gospel writers, but it will resonate with the reality of your life. Mark doesn't deny the beauty or reality of the nativity; however, he seems to believe that Christmas begins—the gospel begins—when Christ intrudes upon the hard realities of life.

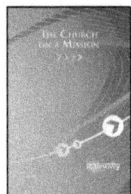

The Church on a Mission

What does it mean to be a church on a mission? The lesson of Acts 1:8 is that we must simultaneously carry out Christ's mandate at home, in our region, in places that have been our blind spots, and around the world.

Colossians
Living the Faith Faithfully

Paul's letter to the Colossians begins with a high-minded philosophical defense of the faith, but concludes with a collection of extremely practical advice for living by faith. This study addresses the questions many Christians face today, helping them apply Paul's practical advice in their own lives.

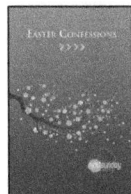

Easter Confessions

Easter confession is often found on many different lips in the Gospel of John. When we listen carefully, those ancient confessions still echo into this new millennium.

Embracing the Word of God

We live during a time of transition in Christian history. Basic assumptions about the truth of the Christian faith are being questioned, not only by nonbelievers, but by Christians themselves. First John offers a starting point for understanding of what it means to "be" Christian.

Esther: A Woman of Discretion and Valor

The book of Esther is not a record of historical facts as such. Rather, it is a magnificent narrative that refuses to interpret life as being driven by coincidence or happenstance. In the otherwise unknown characters of Esther, Haman, and Mordecai, we trace the movement of the divine hand as God collaborates with God's risk-taking people to rescue them from the hand of their enemies.

Facing Life's Challenges

This study explores four significant challenges common to most persons of faith: the challenge of new light, the challenge of time's limit, the challenge of living with mystery, and the challenge of authentic spirituality. Although these issues are neither simple nor easy to ponder, this study effectively leads us in confronting these challenges.

The Four Cardinal Virtues

Christians are learning how to distinguish between members of a church and disciples of Christ. Discipleship involves developing virtues in those who come to our churches seeking life, salvation, grace, mercy. If we want to have something to offer a world in desperate need, then we must return to virtues like discernment, justice, courage, and moderation. We must return to the hard and glorious work of making disciples.

Galatians
Freedom in Christ

Paul wrote with fiery passion, as you will notice from the opening paragraphs of this letter to the Galatians. But his language reveals that he was writing about a crucially important issue—the very nature of salvation in Christ.

A Holy and Surprising Birth

Christmas begins here—discover these five love stories from the book of Luke and renew your appreciation of God's laborious effort to birth our salvation.

How Does the Church Decide?

An array of decisions draw energy and time from church members. These decisions may be theological, such as mode of baptism, aesthetic, such as the color of the sanctuary carpet, or functional, such as the selection of a new minister. This study will consider how the church has made its decisions in the past to help guide our decisions today.

Is God Calling?

Witness the varying forms of God's call, the variety of people called, and the variety of responses. Perhaps God's call to you will become clearer.

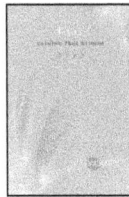

James
Gaining True Wisdom

If we'll be honest with God and ourselves as we study what James says, we can make great strides toward wisdom and a living faith.

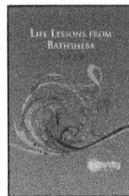

Life Lessons from Bathsheba

Who was Bathsheba? She was a complex figure who developed from the silent object of David's lust into a powerful, vocal, and influential queen mother.

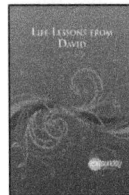

Life Lessons from David

In the Bible, we catch David in the various stages of the human journey: childhood, adolescence, adulthood, and senior adulthood. From the biblical treatment of the stages of David's life, we can land some insights to assist us in better understanding the human journey.

The Matriarchs

The matriarchs of Genesis offer their lives as a testimony of faith, perseverance, and audacity. We learn from their mistakes and suffering. We will gain the hope of Hagar, the joy of Sarah, and the audacity of Rebekah as we are challenged to examine our prejudices and our insecurities while studying Esau and Jacob's wives.

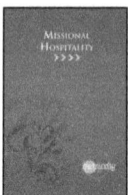

Missional Hospitality

If we are serious about following Jesus, we will be people of open hearts, open hands, and open homes. In other words, as followers of Jesus we will practice the fine art of hospitality. In lesson one, we reflect on hospitality to strangers. In lesson two, we address hospitality to the poor. In lesson three, we focus on hospitality to sinners. In lesson four, we learn about hospitality to newcomers. Lesson five reminds us about our hospitality to Christ.

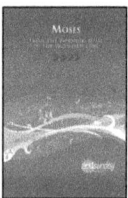

Moses
From the Burning Bush to the Promised Land

We would do well to trace the life of Moses so we might discover how his life changed, both personally and as Israel's leader, as he learned what it meant to love God with all his heart, soul, and strength.

Old Testament Promises to God

Some individuals may feel that our promises couldn't possibly mean anything to God. Perhaps the real question is this: under what circumstances should or do we make such promises? The Old Testament contains several examples of people making promises to God, using the unique form of a biblical "vow."

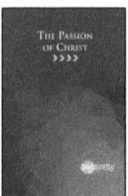

The Passion of Christ

The four lessons in this unit highlight the faith struggles of the early disciples. In lesson one, Jesus addresses the issues of faith and practice. In lesson two, we meet Judas who, like us, struggled with God's Kingdom and human kingdoms. In lesson three, the issue of temptation reminds us that our faith journey is a constant challenge. Lesson Four invites us to remember Peter's experience of "faith failure." Peter's failure, however, is not the final word. There is forgiveness.

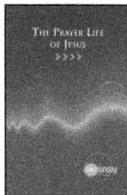

The Prayer Life of Jesus

The study of Jesus' prayer life can deepen our own prayer practices. These five sessions examine the importance of prayer at various stages of Jesus' life and ministry. He made no important decisions without consulting God.

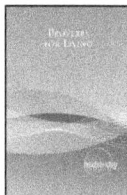

Proverbs for Living

Long ago, a collection of wise teachers committed themselves to the ways of God and collected this wisdom into what we know as the book of Proverbs. These four lessons explore the simple truth of Proverbs: there is a good life to be had—a life lived in faithfulness to God.

Qualities of Our Missional God

Too often we are tempted to let "numbers" drive missions. The book of Numbers reminds us that missions is motivated by something deeper. Missions reflects the heart and nature of God. If we can just get past the math, we can see God's nature clearly in the book of Numbers. . . in the wilderness.

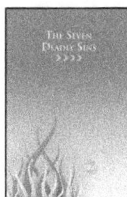

The Seven Deadly Sins

What exactly is sin? Just as we organize our cupboards and our schedules to make sense of our lives, Christian thinkers have organized sin into a number of categories in order to understand and surrender these patterns to God. The notion of "seven deadly sins" emerged as a way to recognize specific dangers to our spiritual lives. The purpose of the book is to guide people away from sin and into a wise and godly life.

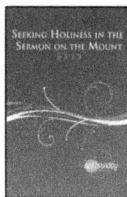

Seeking Holiness in the Sermon on the Mount

The Sermon on the Mount has long been recognized as the pinnacle of Jesus' teaching. But with this importance in mind, it's easy to think of Jesus' teachings as lofty and idealistic, offering little guidance for everyday life. Perhaps Jesus' sermon allows us to see beyond ourselves, beyond our own failures and shortcomings—revealing God's intention for our lives.

Spiritual Disciplines
Obligation or Opportunity?

The spiritual disciplines help deepen a believer's faith and increases his or her intimacy with Christ. In this study, we take a deeper look at some of the disciplines and consider their practice as a response to God's love.

Stewardship
A Way of Living

Great News! Stewardship is not about money! At least not *just* about money. Certainly, stewardship relates to money, and, yes, we need to tithe. However, stewardship branches out into multiple areas of life. Properly practiced, this act of service can lead to peace and purpose in living.

The Ten Commandments

When the Ten Commandments are in the news, it is usually because a judge or teacher has hung them up on the walls. The Ten Commandments do not need to be posted or even preached nearly so much as they need to be practiced and viewed as life-giving, joyful affirmations of a better way of life.

War, Peace, and the Bible

As people of faith, we are faced daily with an expectation that we participate in violent actions, our willingness to allow violence in the world to continue, and our response to violence in our lives. Is there a place for war and violence in our faith?

What Would Jesus Say?
A Lenten Study

To address what Jesus would say, we need to discover what Jesus did say. These lessons will attempt to help us understand Jesus' teachings and apply them today.